The Bunnies' Book of
Seasons

By Sandy DeWitt
Adapted from the original text by Sarah Leslie
Illustrated by Aurelius Battaglia

Platt & Munk, Publishers • New York
A division of Grosset & Dunlap

Previously published as *Seasons*.

SPRING

Spring is here! The bunnies are excited. All around them flowers are blooming. The leaves are budding on the trees. Newborn baby birds are chirping. And it's getting warmer every day.

It is time for the bunnies
to come out of their snug
winter houses, put away
their warm winter coats,
and play in the sunshine.
On a fine spring day,
bunnies like to fly kites,
roll in the grass, and smell
spring flowers…*mm-m-m-m*!

Sometimes there's a spring shower. It might come all of a sudden. Then the bunnies put on their yellow rain slickers and blue galoshes. They like to make mushy mud pies with nice squishy mud and splash in lovely deep puddles.

When it isn't raining, busy bunnies work in their gardens. They grow flowers and herbs and carrots and lettuce and ever so many good things to eat. Bunnies who don't like to work in the garden watch everything from behind the wooden fence.

SUMMER

Summertime! School is out. The sun beats down all day. The days are long and the nights are short. Long sunny days are good for things that grow in the garden.

They are also good for the special outdoor things that bunnies like to do. They play tennis in the lettuce leaves and sunbathe in the carrot patch. Sometimes they have a picnic lunch.

The hot summer sun makes bunnies sleepy.
Napping in the shade of a large lettuce leaf
is a good way to keep cool. Some bunnies
put on a sun hat and read a good book.

Other bunnies like to go swimming to cool off.
They put on their bathing suits and practice
diving into the lake. That's the best place to play
ball on sunny summer days.

FALL

Fall is here! There's a nip in the air. Everywhere the leaves are changing color. The last of the vegetables in the garden are ripe and ready for picking. Oops. Someone has piled too many pumpkins into his barrel.

The squirrels gather
acorns to last them all
winter. The ducks fly
south to warmer places.
And the bunny boys and
girls go back to school.

The bunnies get out their warm sweaters and jackets. The wind blows and the leaves begin to fall. It's time to rake the leaves into piles and pick apples from the trees. The bunnies must be careful not to let any apples fall on someone's head.

Soon it's Halloween. Little bunnies like to dress up as ghosts and witches and clowns. One bunny wears a funny lettuce costume. A jack-o-lantern burns brightly. The wind howls… *oo-o-o-o-o*! What a spooky sound!

WINTER

Wintertime! Now the bunnies like to stay in their snug winter houses. The trees are bare. The ground is hard. The vegetable garden will be empty until spring.

Br-rrr! It's cold outside. Snow falls. Icicles hang from branches and twigs and even from little bunny noses. The days are short and the nights are long. It's a good time to snooze indoors beside a toasty fire.

When the bunnies go outdoors, they wrap up in their woolies and keep busy. There is plenty to do. Bunnies like to go sledding and ice skating. And they love to make snowbunnies.

There is snowball fighting and snowfort building.
But for one bunny, there is dreaming of spring.
Spring will come again soon.